Kalpvriksha

The way of life through Dharma, Karma and Behaviour

Swetha Narsagoal

BookLeaf Publishing

India | USA | UK

Made with ❤ on the BookLeaf Publishing Platform
www.bookleafpub.in
www.bookleafpub.com

Dedication

To Radha Krishn,

When I need him the most he is always there for me as a teacher, friend, protector, guide and much more. The one who taught me the importance of Dharma, Karma and Behaviour.

Preface

" Jo Kachu Kina Tu Kina,
Main Kachu Kina Nahi "

I believe that its always his grace and faith that inspires
me to do everything.
So my poetry is also the blessing of the divine Krishn.

Acknowledgements

To Radha Krishn, who are the supreme, the best teacher, friend, philosopher and guide.The one who is the epitome of love, light and more.

To Shiv Parvati, who are the greatest of the all. The eternal one who are full of strength, oneness and divinity.

To my grandfather, grandmother and my father who have now become the guiding light from the swargalokha. They have always inspired, loved and blessed me in various ways.

To my guru's from my educational institution who shaped my thoughts and way of being.

To my mother, sister, brother and friends who remind me everyday that you are loved beyond measures.

1. Nurturing the beauty of the Jungle

When the cow sat in the fields with grit and calmness,
It's aware of its worth as the supreme being of greatness.

When the peacock danced away in the beauty of rain,
The magnificent colours of rainbow blessed us with
detailing like a vein.

When the sound of jumping deer's felt like steps of tap
dance,
The floor of the jungle turned into the valour of vance.

When the innocence of the baby elephant oozed out
while bathing under the river falls,
The parent elephant's heart filled with joy and peace like
a galore of emotions overall.

When the leaves of the trees blushed in the glory of
greenery,

The sun shined the brightest over the blooming flowers making beautiful scenery.

2. Sensing through the nature

In the stillness of the mind,
In the nothingness of the grind,
In the awareness of the mankind,
In the comforting breeze of wind,
Speaks the nature in your ears
showing the truth that is aligned

The brightest stars of light that shined,
The path of unbelievable magic which streamlined,
The universes which are effortlessly inter twined,
The faith of knowledge that was mined,
See the nature through your eyes,
which is showing the truth that is aligned.

3. Yoga being the source for sacred spiritual growth and wellbeing

Yoga being the narrative of immeasurable potential with
great reverence,
Yoga being the source of spiritual growth with
widespread knowledge,
Yoga being the quiet way of transforming the body, mind
and soul,
Just take that one more step towards enlightenment,
Walk that extra mile for sacred experiences through
alignment.

Attaining mindfulness with stillness and dhyana,
Awakening blissful aura with every pranayama,
Attributing to pure & clean energy for holistic wellbeing,
Just take that one more step towards state of harmony,
Walk that extra mile for changing lives remarkably.

In the serenity of breath to uplift the natural state of

being,
In the physical postures of yoga that inspires to build a
fit & healthy body,
In the veda's & traditions that sailed through time and
age,
Just take that one more step towards the brilliance,
Walk that extra mile with humility and resilience.

4. The nature's wisdom and its way

The sky that's all over watching us hold on even when it
feels like giving up,
The water that shows you the path of integrity while
flowing through the mountains,
The melody of values aligning with the truth that guides
towards honesty.

The fire that shatters away the fears and lets us finally
receive insights,
The moon that brightens your heart with love, light and
pure energy,
The sun that shines and makes you flourish in the
brightness of its wisdom.

The air that clears the fog of uncertainty which helps to
rise above doubts,
The fireflies that bloom graciously ignoring the limiting
beliefs,
The space that dissipates the shadow of ego and spreads

the embracing empathy.
The earth which gives the solid foundation to rebuild
higher and stronger.

5. By the blessings of you supreme Radha Krishn

By the presence of you the awareness established
naturally,
The faith in you grows immensely,
The path always shows itself perfectly,
Eternal one the greatest of all,
It's always been you the supreme radha krishn.

By the teachings of your knowledge wisdom evoked
with grandness,
The bliss of being in love and fondness,
The power of worth, charm and kindness,
The importance of spiritual existence and devotedness,
Affectionate one the dearest of all,
It's always your zeal that's been cherished.

By the virtue of you one discovers the framework for
fulfilment,

You are the confidence, all that's needed to grow and
glow,
You are the inspiration, all that's needed to better
oneself,
You are the brightest light, all that's needed to shine in
the whole wide world,
Righteousness one the smartest of all,
It's always your moral values that shapes the world.

By the force of you one learns the vastness of karma and
free will accurately,
Cumulative karma shaping the forthcoming destiny
accordingly,
Chosen by the divine to mirror highest good bestowing
on their progeny willingly,
Esteemed one the whimsical of all,
It's always your wonders that we behold.

By the blessings of you we understand the need of the
hour,
By the grace of you we realise the power of happiness
and potential,
Courageous one the elevated of all,
It's always your gaze of bravery to face the known and
unknown.

6. The cycle of seasons that enrich you

The mornings you wake up to the peaceful sun gazing
that communicates the power of truth,
The evenings you look up to with soft breeze of air that
calms the wandering thoughts,
The afternoons which are filled with moments of efforts
without attachment but with belief.

The rains that's soothing which eventually quiets down
the overthinking,
The winter that indicates the value of rearranging the
rage by pleasant nature,
The summer that has the capacity to heal,transform and
enrich your inner light.

The days when thought projects what lies within us and
the memory trying to surface,
The months of hardwork that makes the present
beautiful and future worth it,

The weeks that reflects the perseverance as you believe in the magic and timing of divine.

7. Trinity to evolve

Creator of the wisdom for the spiritual, physical and
emotional growth,
Destroyer of the imbalance hidden in limitations that
stops you,
Protector of peace with silence to lead and succeed.

Creator of the stillness to observe, adapt and grow,
Destroyer of arrogance and panic mechanism created by
anxiousness,
Protector of creative ability to shape your future that
brings satisfaction.

Creator of the purpose and guiding us to build the
mindset to fulfil it,
Destroyer of the obstacles and false narratives that bind
you behind,
Protector of pure and true heart eventually which are
favoured by god.

Creator of the urge to be in the present moment and to

know its significance,
Destroyer of the uneasiness created by the stress of the
over doing,
Protector of the outcome by teaching the ability to make
it happen.

Creator of the divine focus and aura that surrounds us,
Destroyer of doubts and despair that dwells under the
shadows,
Protector of intuition and vision that paves the path to
succeed.

Creator of the reality that gets revealed itself gently,
Destroyer of illusion that we still cling upon
unknowingly,
Protector of past, present and future with coherence.

8. Entrusting oneself to the Gods will and wish (Atmapranidhana)

Grateful for gods fingerprint that guides each and every path,
Entrusting oneself to god's wish and avoiding resistance by handing over to god's will,
Only then you observe the wonders he wished upon us without any frills.

Guides you through right direction that leads to the path of awakening and balance,
Gifts you the intuition so sharp to show the purpose and reason that fills you with delight,
Grants you the sthithapragya that fades away the limiting belief when true devotion shines bright.

Observe your calmness with which you work to receive the showering grace,
Be quiet and still enough to sense the vivid visions and

key phrase,
The signs the divine shows almost every day, its no
coincidence in anyways.

9. Awareness

Know the energy you carry upon & the one that
surrounds you,
Know the emotions you are dealing with & the one's that
are being suppressed by you,
Know the patterns that are repeating in various ways &
disturbing you,
Know the way you react to various circumstances and its
impact on you,
Know the reason behind the restless feeling emerging in
when things go slow,
Know exactly how you feel only then its possible to
resolve it to be an improved version of yourself.

10. Acceptance

Accepting the reality that changes skilfully the way of
your perspective,
Guiding force that reshapes you to be the spark that
disrupts, inspires and transforms.

It only gets worse and untameable when emotions get
suppressed,
So be aware and heal the emotion that sits underneath
the mask of pretence.

The act of choosing peace over proving a point,
Refusing to be swayed away by the opinions of others
upright.

Old patterns resurfacing again and again till
acknowledged,
So face it, heal it & then release it so that it dissipates.

Being in synchronicity to quiet down the overthinking,
Moving with intellect to ingrain a solid foundation.

11. Forgive some, Forget some and Face some of the patterns

Forgive the one's, who have transformed enough to make a difference,
Forgive the one's who's intent were genuine by analysing them wisely before doing so,
Forgive the one's who regain authenticity by swallowing the ego,
Forgive the one's who make the efforts to change for the dignity,
Forgive the one's who have the wisdom of not repeating same pattern and mistake.

Forget the stormy pressure that weighs you down unnecessarily,
Forget the clinging one's who only create twisted tales of thoughts,
Forget the one's who initiate triggers knowingly and the pain they caused,

Forget every ounce of irrelevant behaviour since good
mindset is whats required,
Forget the ones who build lies behind you and try to
drain your energy.

Face some since these need a clearing so don't just mask
them up,
Face some as these patterns need to be revised for
growth as a comeback,
Face some as they act as a catalyst for you to bounce
back like a boomerang,
Face some as its essential to get freed from fear, as it's
just a hindrance in the way of prosperity,
Face some as rediscovering your worth is important
more than anything else.

12. Embrace the reign of strength & honesty

The ancestral memory that refers to the reign of strength
& honesty,
Remembering forgotten hearts who always knew way
too much.

Embrace the spiritual gifts by channelling them for
better of all good,
Precognitive dreams and vision that foretell the future as
reflection of the choices made.

Recollect the contribution of the one's who's concern
that mattered the most,
Who overcame the painful void to give the resources we
need.

Symphony in motion that states the rejoice of turning
the tide for liberation,
Spare a thought for the greatness they showered upon us
by their determination.

Ripples of the energies that flows beneath to make us
courageous enough,
Hold the people in memories with regards who defied
the storm through their fortitude.

13. Honour the ancestor

Face your challenges to free an ancestor who was made
to suppress theirs,
Mend the emotions that weren't healed & got passed on
apparently.

Even though we tend to say that we won't repeat the
unhealed ancestral behaviours,
Depth of the existence of ancestral genetics sometimes
results in doing the similar things.

Articulate the cycles which only happens through
conscious awareness,
Anchor your actions in such a way that it dissolves the
barriers of broken one's.

Eventually breaking the curses that needs to be backed
up by the perspective we choose,
Awaken your innate self to know the family triggers that
got build up upon the various generations.

Acknowledge them and release the emotions , struggles
that earlier clans stumbled upon,
Honour the pattern with gratitude and healing,
eventually releasing your entire lineage.

14. Its about remembering the things that matter the most

Its about remembering to design a lifestyle that entails
peace, authenticity and purpose,
Its about remembering to level up by the choices and
changes you make,
Its about remembering that real luxury is
confidence,consistency and alignment.

Its about remembering how the child in you dreamed
and created with utmost faith and effort,
Its about remembering that the right moment is always
now to make the move and reach the goal,
Its about remembering to stop pulling the chords so hard
that it tangles the means.of connection.

Its about remembering that we are held by an unseen
divine force through the rhythm of life,
Its about remembering that it's the solution which needs

to be focused upon and not the problem originated,
Its about remembering that the divine chooses those
who are ready to walk the path with sincerity
and unwavering faith.

15. Every step of choice

Every step that reflects inwards, leads to bloom
beautifully outwards,
Every dream that keeps you awake at night needs you to
go that extra mile,
Every spiritual sign which is a response for your
whispered prayer,
Every blessing makes you shine like a star with pure
intent and powerful purpose,
Every vision that becomes the reality indicates that the
divine is by your side the whole time,
Every challenge faced with stability and simplicity will
only empower you in various ways,
Every new step taken with balanced and controlled mind
is the path for rising of true self,
Every time dharma declines the protectors rise in glory
of the higher power,
Every decision that changes confrontation into
conversation brings clarity.

16. Rise in power through glimmers

You being the most profound gift of nature,
You got to dive a little deeper into your own strength
and stature.

Step up to rise in power through the glimmers,
Stop the act of whining caused by the triggers.

Experiences are the lessons of wisdom to learn from,
Respond accordingly by accepting few and others to
overcome.

Being selective and wise of your words and behaviour,
Being smart enough to know who deserves your
explanation.

The efforts that elevate you and overflow with joy,
The ground strengthened by gallant courage,maturity
and valour.

17. She is fully aware with gratitude

She's fully aware by the fact of being divinely protected
at every altitude,
She's got the faith that's the greatest blessing as
construed,
She knows of her being god's favourite child with full of
gratitude,
She's got the playlists for every mode and magnitude,
She's beautiful inside out with mesmerising personality
and great aptitude.

18. Bandwidth of endearment

When you make every day feel blissful,
that's when you know the frequency matched out.

When you organically blend into each other's values and
goals,
that's when you know the vibration amplified out.

When the power of balanced thoughts you hold
exhibited,
that's when the magnetism that you carry signalled out.

When the unconditional love got acknowledged by the
respect and purpose,
that's when the cosmic connection built and flourished
out.

19. The only way forward

The only way forward is through healing & getting out
of the circling lessons,
The only way of overall well being is embracing the
yesterday, growing today for a beautiful tomorrow.

The only way to succeed is the discipline and
consistency with which you communicate,
The only way forward is by having strength to endure
the hardest times along with good attitude.

The only way of awakening is by knowing the truth,
purpose and living it fully,
The only way of evolving is making god as first priority
and his beautiful force of love that builds the world.

20. There is no need to entertain unnecessary drama

There is no need to entertain the drama created by the manipulators,
since its the reflection of the insecurities they carry from their past bitter experience.

There's no need to soak up the malicious behaviour of the egocentrics,
since its the reflection of their emptiness & bitterness.

There's no need to consume the hate given by others,
since its the reflection of their wounds which they never learnt to handle.

There's no need to hold onto the reactions given by the people in arrogant way,
since its the reflection of unknown burdens they carry upon.

There's no need to imbibe disruption created by the
confused individuals,
since its the reflection of their envy caused by the bruise
they had.

There's no need to squander your time on explaining to
those who trigger you,
since its the reflection of their fears,which they try
imposing to prove invalid point.

21. Rebuild with integrity

Wiping the tears, facing the fears and then watching
eventually how the uncertainty clears,
speaking with clarity, guiding actions with wisdom to
claim the much needs happiness.

Drifting away from the hindering ones with much
needed boundaries,
articulating the intentions and amplifying the strength to
be profoundly content.

Face the distraction and diversion that tries to trap you
in the illusion,
rebuild yourself into the one you dreamed of by making
the illusions to fall apart.

Be true to the nature by knowing what you truly
deserve,
Evolve with moral values that mould you and sparkles
the path with clarity.